# Wonder Wheel

# Wonder Wheel

poems

Harriet Shenkman

GRAYSON BOOKS
West Hartford, Connecticut
graysonbooks.com

Wonder Wheel
Copyright © 2023 by Hariett Shenkman
Published by Grayson Books
West Hartford, Connecticut
ISBN: 979-8-9888186-1-8
Library of Congress Control Number: 2023917412

Cover image: istockphoto.com/@andreka
Book and cover design by Cindy Stewart
Author photo by Jordana Shenkman

# Acknowledgments

I am grateful to the editors of the following journals, where some of these poems previously appeared, often in different versions or with different titles: *Alexandria Quarterly, Berru Poetry Series, The Comstock Review, Evening Street Review, Jewish Currents, Jewish Magazine, Jewish Quarterly, Main Street Rag, Oyez Review, Persimmon Tree, Pink Panther Magazine, Quartet Journal, Sunlight Press, Third Wednesday, VerseWrights, The Westchester Review, Fig Tree Press* and *Thimble Literary Magazine.* I am also grateful to Finishing Line Press, where some of these poems appeared in my chapbooks, *Teetering* (2014) or *The Present Abandoned* (2020).

I am forever thankful to all the poets and teachers who have read drafts of my work and provided encouragement: Jennifer Franklin and the Hudson Valley Writers Center students, the poets Suzanne Cleary, Alicia Suskin Ostriker, Mary Gilliard, Sean Singer, Laura Kasischke, and H.E. Fisher. Members of the Poetry Community of the Scarsdale Library gave me invaluable feedback and provided a supportive community. And most recently, Lynn Melnick at the 92nd Street Y was a savvy and encouraging editor.

I appreciate the JCC of Mid-Westchester, Scarsdale Temple, Dobbs Ferry, Chappaqua and Scarsdale Public Libraries, the Transition Network, the Women's National Book Association and the Hudson Valley Writers Center for giving me the opportunity to share my work in their venues. I am also thankful for the opportunity to serve as Poet-in-Residence at the JCC of Mid-Westchester.

Finally, I am deeply grateful for my loving family, Ethan, Hartley, Jordana and their spouses Jen and Adam. And I absolutely adore my granddaughters, Ari and Mia, whose love and potential inspire me.

for Ari and Mia

*The deaf don't believe in silence.*
*Silence is the invention of the hearing.*

—Ilya Kaminsky

# Contents

# C'mon, Baby

# C'mon, Baby

Me and Chubby Checker
born in the same year
Carmen Miranda wore fruit hats

        and Hitler declared "The Final Solution."

His mama in Spring Gully
fixing grits, mine in Flatbush
dusting the blinds.

        Amniotic fluids flood the floors

while across the ocean
in my mother's Ukrainian town
her sisters are herded into the woods.

        Cords severed, lungs expanded

our cries pierce the air
me and Chubby
defying the Aryan strain,

        C'mon, Baby   C'mon.

# My Only Clue

My mother had a missing left big toe.
I watched her stuff a wad of cotton

into the foot of her stocking
pull the hose up to her thigh

and straighten the long black seam.
She never said how the toe went missing.

I imagined it stuck in an animal trap
chopped off by marauding Cossacks

beset by a black crusty disease.
Annihilation was in the air like pollen,

but such things were not for a child to know.

# Empty Goblets

In the town where my mother was born
roosters strutted in the yard. Her deaf sisters

      could not hear them crowing.

They gestured in signs. She played the piano.
They pretended to be the audience.

      Later, the mobile killing units arrived.

Across the ocean, four empty goblets
sat on our Seder table. No other children

      to help search for the broken shard of matzo.

We left the door open, poured wine in a silver goblet
for Elijah, hoping he would enter and drink,

      a sign the world was redeemed.

# Sign Language

Two fists spring open, fingers spread stiff
palms inward, eyes wide open

        a voiceless scream

I can't imagine   Just can't imagine
how they stood naked

        before a sodden pit

Tears may have streamed down their gaunt faces
Maybe one deaf sister clutched the arm of

        the next in line

Did they read the lips of the Ukrainian police
shouting to bring their belongings, now

        piled on the ground?

Did they close their eyes and feel the wool fabric
between their fingers, fabric they sewed

        on their black Singers?

Maybe one sister imagined lying beside another
warming her corpse

        in the cold earth?

I know they never did watch me bounce
my Spalding ball in our Brooklyn courtyard

# Lost in Egypt

"Where are you going, to *Mizraim*?"
my father would ask, invoking the desert

my ancestors wandered for over forty years.
He meant, don't get lost on the BMT line,

smooch under the boardwalk, get stuck
in the air on the Wonder Wheel.

Years later, a voice whispers in my head,
 "Don't get lost in *Mizraim*."

Meaning the wilderness of the unseen self
where we teeter between light and dark.

# Our New Year

On the Jewish New Year, we dressed
in our finery, my mother in her
hand-made dress with lace collar, father
in a worn jacket, and me
in a skirt and blouse bought off-the-rack.
We strolled the Brooklyn boardwalk,
nodded to people we knew.
No Temple for us.
That was for rich people
who lived in private houses.
No lighting candles on *Shabbos*
pressing our lips to the Torah
reciting a prayer for healing, though
we could have used it.
*God helps those who help themselves*,
my father said, remembering
his own father in prayer all day
while his five children
felt gnawing in their stomachs.

# Unrequited Love

She sang her siren-song bent over
a black Singer, knee at the metal lever.

She tried to lure me
with mother-daughter outfits,

a flowered midriff, matching skirt,

a princess-waist wool jumper
velvet bow beneath the bust,

a raised polka-dotted dress,

a magenta-red sheath
slits down either side

But I spurned her advances
for clothes off-the-rack

like the other girls had.

# Infraction

My first time in the principal's office.
Long windows and an immense desk, a world map
behind his bald head, my mother bewildered,

a tiny figure in a polished oak armchair.

I was summoned for harassing Mrs. Mendelsohn,
our fifth-grade teacher. She was squat
with wire-rimmed glasses, grey hair chopped at the ear.

I can't remember my infraction.

Not paying attention, maybe?
Questioning her facts, snickering at her pointed finger
and flesh-colored stockings. Her old-lady shoes?

I was, it seems, the ringleader.

I sensed her lack of confidence, the other children's scorn.
Now, nearly Mrs. Mendelsohn's age, I apologize.
I apologize, but she has passed on,

and I'm haunted by what I am capable of.

# That Liminal Space

Out the window, I stared
at the neighbor's undershirts
hanging stiffly on the clothesline.
A round fluorescent light shone
down on the Formica table
in our canary-yellow kitchen.
My father at one end,
celebrated a ripe cantaloupe,
my mother at the other end
bemoaned the weather,
me, wanting to run outside and play
with a little sister I didn't have.
She looks up at me now
from that liminal space
between absence and not being born.
I learned years later, my mother rode a taxi
to an address scribbled on a slip of paper
opened her thighs
squeezed her eyes shut
and rid herself
of a baby they could not afford.

# Juicy Fruit

1

She counts chimneys high up
over the elevated train tracks until all the sweetness
is sucked out of her sticks of Juicy Fruit.
*Where are we going?*
*You'll see,* her father says.

They arrive at a red brick building.
*Here are your pajamas, put them on.*
When she turns around, her father is gone.

2

She sits on a board between two chairs.
Locks of hair drop to the floor.
Buster Brown in the barber's mirror, she thinks.
*It's not me.*

3

The children slurp milk and spoon food into their mouths.
The matrons, Holocaust survivors, hover.
*Eat, think of the starving children in Europe.*

She stares at her plate night after night, the globs
of egg yolk, peas, meat. She cannot eat her aloneness.

No one says her mother is in a T.B. sanitorium.

She tiptoes across the room, stuffs a clump of beef behind
the radiator. The next night, a crumbled cupcake, a banana.
She feeds the radiator
until the iron coils give off a putrid smell.

The matrons rail against vermin, but understand despair.

4

She climbs the steps to the attic room to visit her doll.
The matron is propped up by pillows,
one leg in a white cast.
She lets her touch the cold hard plaster.

5

She dreams of sticks of Juicy Fruit.
Chewing and chewing out all the sweetness.

6

Her mother appears one Sunday, holds out
a pair of shiny Mary Janes.
She pulls off her brown high-tops. Walks up and down
in her patent leather shoes.
"Why are you limping?" her mother asks.

*There is no cause,* the doctors say.
*No cause.*

# The Last Night of Channukah

Eight candles burning, tender wicks glowing
atop the refrigerator.
Home alone, twisting to Chubby Checker,
her thumps shake the tiny kitchen
and topple three candles. They fall
behind the fridge where her mother stores beach chairs.
Flames rise and lick the walls.
She flings saucepans of water until
burly firemen lugging hoses and axes arrive.
Her mother walks in
to a floor and ceiling blackened in soot,
chairs charred and chopped into pieces,
not the eight-day miracle they meant to celebrate.
Her mother snarls, hair like coiled snakes.
She runs from the apartment,
wanders the streets, wondering
why her mother didn't say,
*Thank God you weren't hurt,*
though she must have meant it.

# Arthur Knew

Arthur was tall and he knew
how his parents *did it*.

He led her down the steps to the alley between
our brick buildings, cans of ash

      lined up like drunken sentinels.

He pressed her up against the yellow brick.
She felt his taut body, his dragon breath,

      her heart beating like a rebel clock.

"Like-this," he whispered.

But when he looked up at the windows
four stories up, blinds half raised,

      he mumbled, *never mind*.

She watched his lanky figure bound up the steps,
two at a time,

      not knowing

whether to be disappointed
or relieved.

# Serpentine Ride

She rode the Wonder Wheel
with a boy wearing a studded leather jacket,
hair slick in a ducktail.
She feared being locked up with him,
150 feet above the Atlantic, no one
to hear her scream.
She imagined his muscled arm pulling
her close, his smoky breath, having his way
with her up in the air.
They swung on the serpentine track
toward the hub of the wheel,
and out to the edge of the circle.
A momentary thrill as they lingered
over the ocean
the balmy summer breeze
a sprinkling of stars
the boy harmless
her shudder of disappointment.
She held onto the rail,
swinging from fear to awe
as they glided to the bottom,
landing on the sidewalk
where a gaggle of children
screamed for more cotton candy.

# The Looker

Honey Plotkin had lashes thick with mascara,
face heavy with pancake makeup.
She had a way of walking
that inspired the boys. *She's a looker*, they would say.
Her powers eluded
us seventh-grade girls. She hoarded
the secrets we longed to share.
Rumor was Honey went off
and had an unexpected baby.
She might have been a heroine
in an Elena Ferrante novel, but she lived
in a Brooklyn walkup far from Naples.
I wish I knew what befell Honey in later life.
Maybe she married a trucker
and raised five brawling brats or started
a global cosmetics empire?  Maybe
she became a Jehovah's Witness?
What if she put pen to paper
and voiced
our most forbidden desires?

# First Love

In sixth grade English, Mrs. Kaminsky ruled.
I loved a boy three seats away
who failed to notice me. He was pale
from having had scarlet fever,
though I imagined him a brooding poet.
We lived near the ocean and wrote odes
to Poseidon, god of the sea.
My first love moved on from P.S. 215.
He grew up to have his voice and image
on countless TV screens until
he was shunned for luring women
into hotel room closets
and biting their bare backs.
Not the bard whom I imagined, yet
he still ignored me
at our chance encounter
in the check-in line at La Guardia airport.
I stared at his back, wondering.

# Reverence

My father hid fifty-dollar bills
in an Oxydol box under the kitchen sink
though we revered The Lincoln Savings Bank.

I whispered in the marble-lined interior,
President Lincoln carved into the façade.

Our next most sacred institution
was Mrs. Stahl's Knishes, caddy corner to the bank,

worshipped for its potato pocketed in crisp layers of dough.
My father brought home a bulging paper bag,

no mention of his oldest sister sentenced to the gulag,
soup made of potato peels for her meal,

or his other sister and her two children forced
onto a freight train headed to a death camp.

I tore open the filled brown bag. He favored the kasha
and I, the slightly sweet cherry cheese.

# The Best There Is

My father bent over a bowl of blueberries,
a piece of salty herring,
*The best there is.*

We watched Betty Grable and Dan Dailey movies.
Munched corned beef on rye sandwiches
in the dark theatre.

In his old age, he believed he was escaping
through the woods, and we found crusts of bread
under his pillow in the morning.

# Rio Uncle

Sugar Loaf rose above the sea
San Cristo stretching his arms

to bless the city at dusk.

Father's brother landed in Rio, hid out in
Copacabana, disguised as a poet, wanted

for killing a Cossack with a rock.

He wore a white suit,
spectator shoes, a white handkerchief

in his breast pocket.

The woman he married painted a beauty mark
above her lip, flung a full plate of feijoada

across the table at him.

He came to visit us in Brooklyn, left pee
on the toilet seat, gave me

a doll with blinking eyelids

I tucked her in at night. Watched
her lashes close over lacquered cheeks.

# School Photo

My mother learned French and geography
in a Polish gymnasium,

though I never heard her utter a word of French

or recite the names of continents and rivers.
I found a torn sepia photo of her,

three young men in suits on either side.

She went to school with the boys,
but no man would marry her,

family deafness, a curse they believed.

My mother scraped together money for one passage
on a ship leaving to any open port.

She worked in a garment factory,
not what she dreamed of in her feather bed,

roosters crowing in the yard.

After ten years, she met my father.
*I like to listen to the Overture of 1812,* he said,

and she replied, *Two can live as cheaply as one.*

# Coney Island Break-Up

Mother dunked her tea bag
until the boiling water was barely yellow.

She longed for a front-stooped home,
a conversation about the world.

She complained about the price of lamb chops,
the fishy smell of the ocean, the damp weather.

He sewed midsole to bottom, came
from the shoe factory stinking of leather.

*Only a game,* he said, when he lost at gin rummy.
He was the joker at the card game.

For many winters, she pointed a silver reflector
toward the sun, and one January she took off for good.

*I see said the blind man,* he said, and went
to walk the boardwalk all the way to the Parachute Jump.

# The Wedding Tale

# The BMT Line

I fled on the BMT line, a long braid
down my back, leather sandals
on my feet,
to a narrow railroad flat,
poetry and La Dolce Vita on my mind.
My mother came to visit, tried
to lure me back
with a package of meat, ground twice.
I did not budge
until a guy with hazel eyes turned up.
He knew all the capitals of Africa
and on our first date
listened intently to Thelonious Monk.
Three months later, I proposed
and he said yes.
We rode back over the Brooklyn Bridge
to where the sea air smelled like fish
and the Wonder Wheel
lit up the boardwalk,
the cars sliding back and forth
over the cadenced foam
of the Atlantic.

# The Wedding Tale

The groom glanced down at his shoes
imagining the glass beneath his foot,
the fragility of human relationships

The rabbi had been enlisted as he fed pigeons
outside his window. The wedding canopy,
a prayer shawl strung over four thin poles.

Mother was radiant in aqua organza with white corsage.
The guests assembled, her only cousin and his family
travelling all the way from Buenos Aires.

The rabbi began his Hebrew chanting, eyes closed,
lost in a Babylonian exile. It was a while before
I heard *Aaron*, my father's name, followed

by a muddle of Hebrew prayers.
*I was being married to my father.*
I turned to the groom. He lifted my bridal veil,

his lips brushing my ear, and whispered,
*Screw Freud.* The guest shouted Mazel Tov
and threw handfuls of tiny candies at us.

# Wife

The rumor is Prince Charles, now King,
has his shoelaces ironed.
Your mother ironed your dad's silk undershorts.
I never ironed anything at all, haunted by
my own mother in her flowered apron
bent over a board,
steam iron in hand, stamping
fabric to her will.
I put meatloaf on the table, wiped
my hands on the back of my jeans.
Bought wash-and-wear clothes for our children,
watched them tumble in the dryer.
Instinct led me on a meandering path.
You never complained.
Your shirts came back from the laundry
folded and starched.
I rocked our third infant into the night,
reciting my dissertation outcomes
in a bleary brain.

# Catwoman

You crushed on Michelle Pfeiffer, those
misty green eyes and high cheek bones. You
favored the scene of her sprawled
on the baby grand.
I did not balk, as long as
you came home each night
and loosened your striped tie with a sigh.
As long as you took the boys downtown
to shop for records.
As long as you curled your fingers
as if playing a clarinet,
and tapped your feet to the beat.
When Michelle turned into Catwoman, tempting
the caped crusader with her feline licks,
I did not object. As long as
you laughed
when I swung from gravitas to gaiety
and you admired my disguises.

# Riff One

You grooved to the angular melodies of Monk.

> me, to a gull balancing on one leg.

You explained *sua sponte*. I read

> *The Waste Land* as you dozed.

Sausage biscuit your favorite, mine granola

> for my morning-after fare.

I valued decision. You favored the merits

> of dwelling on a point.

Silence was inspiring to you.

> Me, a chirping jungle bird.

You spread cream cheese on your bagel.

> I flung gobs, the edges rough.

You dreamed of floating on the Dead Sea.

> My fantasy, the Pacific swells.

I craved sticks of Juicy Fruit. You longed

> to puff deeply on a Habano.

I thrilled to the stomp of the Flamenco. You got off

> on the strumming.

I sip a Margarita now, as you down your Jack Daniels, Monk

> striking chords on his piano.

# Bacchanalia

Splashed on my mother's Silent Night toilet water
from the midnight blue bottle, Lenny riffing
on his clarinet across the courtyard of our walkup.
My breasts two fawns like Bathsheba's as she bathed
on the rooftop, I indulged in fantasy.
Ravished by Butch Cassidy,
the sound technician crooning Sinatra.
Mounted by the pinstriped guy in the coat closet.
Dabbed *L'Air du Temps* behind each ear,
lured you from that Valdosta girl, Nina Simone singing
*Don't Smoke in Bed.*
We honeymooned at The Plaza, drove the Chevy
down south to see the world.
My breasts painful,
three infants wailing into the night. We acquired
a house with a brick hearth, a Labrador named Lucy.
Each year, turkey and cranberry sauce on the table,
a slew of birthday candles and buoyant toasts.
And then we were old.
Muggy air under the comforter, my leg over yours,
a toe pressed into your sole.

# Objects

History sends me wandering through our rooms,
pondering objects.

Your mother's silver-plated candelabra,
always needing polishing.

The ceramic jug thrown by the Carolina potter
with arthritic thumbs.

Our Roman style wine goblet, the one
we leave for Elijah each year.

Our granddaughter's drawing of a three-legged camel,
basking under sun and nimbus cloud.

The Mr. Coffee pot, the one that brews
medium roast, the way we like it.

A family photo in a silver frame, the kind of personal item
thrown on bonfires at Quai de la Gare.

Nazis plundered Jewish homes, sent saucepans, light bulbs,
and family curios to Germany on six hundred trains.

I am aching to conclude *no plunder possible*.
That loss of mere objects cannot obliterate us.

# Along the Beach

Along the white sand beach, we gather
a handful of shells,
bleached fossil-like remnants,

bone-dry and carved in petrified swirls,
punctured in patterns
that would please Michelangelo.

They bring to my mind shells cracked open,
ushering a newborn into the light.
And there is the shell

of a rifle's bullet
left after a quick death.
Now, there is the withering that befalls you,

your brain calcifying without mercy.
Miles of sand rimmed by sea and sky
stretch before us.

You turn your shaded eyes toward me.
*Where are we going?*

# If Only

If only the past could stretch before us,
        the wavering future behind.

We saw the birds roosting
        when we toured the Seminole nature preserve,

the eagles resting in nests thick and high up,
        safe from predators.

In Barcelona, we lingered at a café
        and I sipped a cortado.

You marveled at the rounded corners of buildings,
        the terraces with Catalan flags.

The Santa Fe sky awed and enveloped us,
        the land flat and dusty.

At the fair, you bought me an Anasazi shard
        to wear around my neck.

I listened to the whisper of the ancients, a hint of
        what lay ahead.

Later, Georgia O'Keeffe
        spoke to us in watercolor hues.

# Riff Two

You would set the house clocks
explain *due process*
savor my fish stew
admire my suede boots
cradle my secrets
sooth my wounds
I will recite my name in rhyme
turn into a Warhol print
sixteen of me on the bedroom wall
soak your tie in L'Heure Bleue
make you taste my essence in a roux
tattoo my likeness on your arm
because who will I be,
if you can't remember me?

# Pain Relief

I sent you to CVS
for two rolls of toilet paper,
dandruff shampoo, a pint
of vanilla ice cream.

In the hair products aisle,
you stop a blonde
with golden curls,
ask for the best shampoo.

She smiles and points
to a shimmering tube,
invites you to admire her
silky hair in the shower.

Fantasy is your off ramp,
the real world left to me.
At the dairy freezer,
nothing much happens,

but the toilet paper aisle,
another matter.
A man with sidelocks
confronts you, eager to

tie a box with the Torah
on your forehead,
and dance you past antacids
into the pain-relief aisle.

# Happy Nail Salon

*Select color, please.*
*Demure Vixen.* I picture
our first date in Greenwich Village.
*Nice day, no?* The manicurist files,
reaches for my arm and the tube of cream,
the half-minute massage not enough.
*Cut cuticles?* No.
You at the storefront window,
drumming on the glass.
I look away,
not the partner I'd hoped to be.
*Please sit, fifteen minutes to dry.*
On the wall, Van Gogh in a gilt frame.
I gaze into the sunflowers.
How long before he went mad?
*Only six minutes left.*
Your face at the window again.
I spring up,
brush the tabletop with my hand,
a mess of fuchsia streaks now.

# Jazz Buff

You were a jazz buff, Coltrane and
Monk your favorites
Now, you tap out your syncopated beats
on tabletops, dash boards, armrests
You wake up at 3am, scatting nonsense syllables,
rousing me from sleep
You click the quarter notes with your tongue,
your timing impeccable, though you
confuse the days of the week, the months,
the year.

One   Two   Three    Four
Doo—AAAAH!   Doo---AAAAH!

# Dementia Unit

Cappuccino in the bistro
two Lorna Doones each
You devour one of mine
We walk around the building from back door
to parking lot
You play Gin Rummy with your son,
confuse spades with hearts.
He throws out a joker,
*Send in the Clowns* playing in the background…
You shoot pool with our daughter, ignoring the rules.
In the craft room, you are offered
scraps of pastel paper to paste on an Easter basket.
You never once celebrated the birth of Jesus,
but you slant a pink egg over the paper.
Then there are Friday afternoons,
thirty minutes of prayer with an itinerant rabbi.
We pray for healing and for the dead.
I wish there was a prayer about slow withering,
an explanation of the divide
between the infinite and the finite.
And there is my leaving,
each time, a rending.

# Venice

I stood on the Bridge of Sighs

      and grieved,

not for the last glimpse of the city
as prisoners once did, but for a sighting

      of you

as you once were,
clear-eyed, two years over twenty,

      thick presidential hair,

a rosebud in your lapel, eager
to break the glass beneath your foot.

# The Mantle

# The Mantle

I did not discard
the black velvet cloak my mother stitched.
The ripped satin lining
attached with a safety pin,
patches of fabric worn with age.
I dressed in the cloak once at Halloween.
I could have worn it to the opera,
or over a gown at a formal wedding,
but I did not.
It hung in the back of my closet,
a solitary bequest,
brooding like a forlorn child
until I noticed it.
My mother kept silent.
Now, I stitch her silences together
and strut in the velvet mantle.

# I Found a Picture Postcard

S.S. Estonia   Baltic American Line
        a sleek ship   calm waters
Two sturdy smokestacks
        a cloudless sky
My mother sailed   third class
        a young woman   alone
She never spoke of
        roiling seas    the sickness
the family she left behind

Port of entry, Quebec 1929
        a young woman    alone
hoping for a better life
        unaware of   the horror
that would have found her
        had she not sailed

*T.S.S. "Estonia," Baltic America Line*

# Random Hand

The signer stands to one side
of the mayor.          Her hands fly up,

       first to her forehead, then

     to her heart. Her fingers flutter,

         telling of heartbreak,

yet another senseless shooting.

It conjures in me my mother's sisters.
In the town before dawn
the Jews were rounded up,
stripped of their clothes.
Five deep pits dug,
steps carved to ease entry.
I imagine them signing
from an unmarked grave.

My mother knew the random hand of mercy,
and they do not begrudge her.

# Requiem

*Yocha, Chana, Gisye, Rochel*

your beauty only imagined, voices mute,
four ghostly souls at the Seder table.

*Yocha, Chana, Gisye, Rochel*

One bullet to the back of the neck, you fell
like plant stalks into the open ground.

*Yocha, Chana, Gisye, Rochel*

You embroidered blouses and dresses,
each stitch a proclamation.

Where are those garments now? I want
to slip one on, gaze in the mirror, admire

the seams, the finely stitched hems,
dresses brought home by German soldiers

returned from the killing units,
bearing gifts. Dresses forgotten in closets

of wives and sweethearts, bones thinned,
hair wispy, as old as you would have been.

*Yocha, Chana, Gisye, Rochel*

# Inherited Trauma

The child's drawing is of a five-legged camel,
though she insists there are two camels.

The one-humped creature stands under a fierce sun,
five rays reaching toward grey clouds.

The grinning dromedary is ready,
ears alert for a pail of figs or marauding soldiers.

Life's essentials are in the rendering.

Sun, gathering clouds, a hump of provisions,
five spindly legs for running away fast.

# Buenos Aires

I adore the Tango, the smoldering embrace,
                    slow – slow,   quick   quick   quick.

Carlos Gardel singing in the brothels.
La Recoleta, the rich lolling in mausoleums.

My mother's cousin took leave from the Russian army,
came home to a village emptied of Jews.

They waited in line for a bullet to the back of the neck,
                    slow – slow,   quick   quick   quick.

He wrote to my mother. She sent one dollar
in an envelope to an address in Buenos Aires.

Now, I arrive at the entrance to his home, layers
of corpses smoldering between us.

*Yes, your mother's sisters were deaf.  No,*
*no one knew the cause.*

*Yes, they were rounded up with the others.*
*Led to the woods outside of town.*

We embrace, our hearts beat loudly,
                    slow – slow,   quick   quick   quick.

# Moscow, 1989

Behind a quilted apartment door, my father's niece,
weeps for refusing to know her mother

when she returned after years in the gulag,
*An enemy of the people.*

Her mother shoveled coal into furnaces,
recited ingredients for her mama's borscht,

*beets, cabbage, onions, beef, salt, dill*
a magic trick against hunger.

And now in a Moscow church lined with gold,
she and I burn candles for the dead,

and for our good fortune.
She spooned kasha in an orphan home,

and across the Atlantic, I sipped tomato soup,
thick as blood, as the *Einsatzgruppen* marched.

# West of Kyiv, 1989

Only one Jew left in Korzec says the town clerk,
a statue of Lenin out front.

>*my mother's family lived here for 400 years*

The one Jew remembers my family    a sorrel soup
is served, a tablecloth pulled from the clothesline,

>*I stare into the hole in the tablecloth*

He leads us to a blue-doored cottage, my mother's house, dacha
of a Soviet general now. *Nothing changed in the inside,* he says.

>*nothing?*

Before we depart, I offer Schneider two packs of Marlboros.
He rummages in a drawer. With sunken eyes, hands me a photo.

>*a photo of the ravine*

I cannot imagine the faces, just

>*four thumps, a rustle of limbs*

Schneider slips a cigarette between his lips.

>*smoke curls around us*

He flicks ash. *They'll have to send a truck of topsoil,* he says,

>*the bones are coming up.*

# Little Odessa, 2023

Concession stands sell pink cotton candy,
soft drinks, sour *Kvass*.

Cyrillic letters blaze from storefronts.
The boardwalk slats creak underfoot.

Years ago, her father walked the boardwalk,
his bald head daring the noon sun.

Fireworks lit up the sky on Tuesday nights,
bursts of red and yellow, a collective sigh

as streaks of light trickled into the ocean.
Afterward, he danced her to bed to Ukrainian melodies.

Today, ladies with ebony hair and glittering sweaters
shop for the ripest fruits on Brighton Beach Avenue.

They haggle over the best Beluga, trying
not to think of

their Odessa by the Black Sea
bombarded by heavy shelling.

# What If

my mother's sisters had gone instead to St. Sophia's in Kiev
to sew the robes of priests and nuns and pray to Jesus

*What if*

they had bent over their Singers and tailored perfect uniforms
sent them express to Nazi Commanders

*What if*

they had vowed to sew dresses
for wives and sweethearts of soldiers

*Consider*

The hooded men in Charlottsville, Tree of Life Synagogue

*We want to believe in goodness*

Yet, they would still be lined up at the pit's edge,
waiting for a bullet to the back of the neck

# Exodus

"Next year in Jerusalem" we say.
I'm thinking of pulling up stakes, selling the house
giving the housewares and china away.

Joseph dreamed of sheaves of wheat.
Abraham, a flaming torch,
I, of wandering the cobblestones in sandals.

I'd listen to the Muezzin summon worshipers to prayer.
eat falafel dripping with tahini. Touch
the flat of my hand to the Western Wall, squeeze

a slip of paper between the stones. Plead
for the blessings of silence and the end of silence.

I'd gather my courage and ride a one-humped camel
into the desert, me and my sullen-lipped companion,
hoping for a cooling rain.

# Morning at Home Goods

I gravitate toward Home Goods these mornings
pink flamingoes on fragile legs   tulips set in pink stones

Two frogs in double rocking chair, $129.99
male holds up a wine glass   female reads a book

Reminds me of us, not so long ago

Nearby a distressed dining table is set for six
we would have had to add more chairs

Our lives lead us to mourn in unexpected places
me in these overflowing aisles

The linen section is stacked with comforters
we favored the 100% cotton reversible kind

My face multiplies in square and oval mirrors
you behind me with gray-tinged hair

I stop at a giant wall clock, Grand Hotel
printed above its hands, a white tag

off its face. *No Returns Allowed*

# Modigliani Exhibit

I always liked Modigliani's elongated necks,
unseeing eyes and reclining nudes.

Lola, Adrienne and Jeanne gaze at me,
woman to woman,

and you, the ghost hovering.

Music was your love, not paintings,
yet you tagged along when I toured the galleries.

I linger at a portrait of Anna Akhmatova
and stop before the Greek caryatids,

sense you meandering through the rooms.

We were a couple once, part of the admiring crowd,
me, not a stranger envious of the nearby pair,

his hand caressing the nape of her neck, unaware
they are the exhibit.

# Triumphal March

My father's ghost shifts in his seat
waiting for our son's triumphal march.

Awed by the abundance of ivy,
he holds the graduation program up close

*lux et veritas* in tiny print.

After the tassels slide from right to left,
the mortarboards tossed in the air,

we stroll past the giant clock tower,
the statue of Nathan Hale, class of 1773.

My father peers up at the statue,
seeking light and truth.

He stretched leather on a shoe last.
Our son studied Aristotle and Homer.

# The Western Wall

Moss juts from crevices
between the blocks of stone,
insistent,

like the wailing over thousands of years.

A small girl
in a spaghetti strap shirt
chants from the Torah,
fringed shawl covering her shoulders,
a curl peeking
from beneath her yarmulke,
voice melodious,
confident in a language tattered
by ages of use.
Her strap falls. She lifts it,
swipes at the stray curl,
bends over the ancient text.
Her voice surges through the internet
across the ocean to us.

*Hineni.*

*Here I am.*

# A Tendril of Joy

I pour a mug of Dunkin' medium roast.
Dump my terry cloth robe with frayed collar
into the trash. Buy a very-berry lip gloss.
Meet with Rabbi Cohen
about joining the Temple, though
I barely believe in God.
My mother almost fell off the delivery table
with joy when I was born,
but at Mac Levi's dance studio, I refused
to do somersaults.
I hid behind the coal bin in the cellar
when she called to go to class.
I wish I were a sorcerer who could banish regret.
I devour two strawberry mochis, paint
my toenails Fiesta Pink.
Try to sing Piaf's *regrette rien*
though I am badly out of tune. I celebrate
the revival of the espresso martini,
and succumb to a tendril of joy
when I hear a girl I adore scatting uptown.

# The Stroll

The CVS down the street closed
and the grocery with the sweetest tangelos.
Alone now, I talk to strangers.
A man led by a long-eared spaniel,
a couple wheeling twins,
a woman with lidded eyes and a forlorn smile.
Grief is my stealth companion.
I stroll past the bakery that offers
your favorite almond pastries.
At the ballet store window, I imagine
twirling in the pink tutu.
A few doors down, I consider
eyelash extensions.  At the tattoo shop,
a soaring eagle lifts me
and drops me on the sidewalk.
At the corner, I park myself at a café table,
order a chocolate croissant. Attempt
to tally the losses.
I find a ball point pen,
scribble on a paper napkin, interrogate
the umbilical link between loss and love.
Wonder if the tiny sparrow
flitting across my shadow knows.

# Daughter

I lie on the narrow massage table, face down,
shoulders tight. *Marla's strokes*
*are slow, her fingers deep.* My daughter used to
dress in miniskirts and dangling earrings, Madonna
among the fairy princesses.
*You can go deeper, but not too much, Marla.*
She chanted from the Torah at the Western Wall
and drove my car without a license.
*Marla kneads my arms and travels to my fingertips.*
After she passed the bar, I bought her
three pinstriped suits. A District Attorney,
she helicoptered to crime scenes,
a detective's hand on her thigh.
*My lower back is killing me, Marla. Go deep.*
She prosecuted sex crimes.
A gossamer wedding gown, glass broken under foot.
*I almost fall off the narrow table.*
The universe spins on its own inexorable axis.
My mother once stood at the top of the stairs
as I lugged Joan Baez records and my worn Lady Chatterley
down four flights.
She held out a package,
two pounds of chuck, ground twice.

# Lamed Vovniks

I'd like to know the unnamed thirty-six people roaming the earth
the designated **righteous**.

It could be the freckled fifth-grader who plays the tuba
or the topless blonde at the Texas Go-Go bar.

I want to meet these *Tzadiks* at a dinner party
dab my mouth with a napkin and turn to each one.

How do you keep it up? I'd ask.
When you enter a bank, do you keep yourself

from sliding the ballpoint pen into your pocket?
Do you stop to help every beggar on the street?

I want to be the thirty-seventh Lamed Vovnik.
I'll climb mountains and descend into valleys

to search for people who are in mourning
and require a good deed.

I'll spin their grief into gold
and render painless their prickly thorns of guilt.

# Ghost of A Daughter

I wonder if I will die
alone like my mother did.
I flew to a city far
from where she raised me.
She was in her railed bed
wisps of hair spread on her pillow.
I held out my hand,
but she pushed it away.
She stared at the bedrail.
Next morning, I drove for a coffee
and a sausage biscuit, then back.
Still, she refused to know me.
Ghost of a woman
who learned geography and French,
fled a Ukrainian village
and sailed on the S.S. Estonia.
Me, ghost of a daughter
rushing to the airport
for a flight home.

# Natural Disaster

I wanted to live where there are no natural disasters.

No hurricane Andrew, Ian or Victoria
to submerge cars, flood houses
soak clothes and family photos, drown the cat, leave

us wandering in the dark.

No wildfires that ravish the land, fell trees
burn houses, stores, and churches to the ground,
coat every surface with gray ash

and give off acrid smoke to choke on.

No giant roar before
molten lava spills from the mountain top
dormant for years, spewing

volcanic ash over villages below.

Your pained lingering,
a surrender of logic, laughter, bodily functions,
our shared history,

was the disaster we could not escape.

# Wonder Wheel

Our gondola swings over the choppy waters,
150 feet above the Atlantic. It threatens
to spill us out over the eroded beaches

and into the frigid ocean.

We lurch forward but do not tumble,
land back on the ground, nod
to unseen deities

who bestow random mercy

and skip onto another amusement—
a Nathan's hot dog smothered in sauerkraut
an overflowing cup of crinkle-cut fries.

We hear the screams of folks riding
the Cyclone
thrilled to be skirting danger.

As we stroll the boardwalk,
slats creaking underfoot,
we ponder

our tiny existence,

and debate the future of the planet,
eager to prepare ourselves
for the next heady ride.

# About the Author

Harriet Shenkman is the current Poet-in-Residence at the Jewish Community Center of Mid-Westchester. She earned a Ph.D. from Fordham University, an M.Ed. from Duke University, and is a professor emerita at City University of New York. Her poetry awards include the Women's National Book Association Annual Contest and the Women Who Write International Poetry Contest. Her work has appeared in *Westchester Review*, *The Alexandria Quarterly*, *Comstock Review*, *The Berru Poetry Series of the Jewish Book Council*, and elsewhere. Two poetry chapbooks were published by Finishing Line Press. She has read her poetry at libraries, synagogues, the JCC, and other venues. A first-generation American, she was raised in Brooklyn, New York.

www.ingramcontent.com/pod-product-compliance
Lightning Source LLC
Chambersburg PA
CBHW060350130626
46553CB00003B/1167